1

"In Search of a New Morality", 2nd Edition"
By Wolfgang Mack PhD

Published by WAMFAM Press
1301 Spring Street, Suite 28H
Seattle WA, 98104

Images in the text by Wolfgang Mack
or in the public domain

Library of Congress Cataloging-in-Publication Data:
Library of Congress Control Number: 2014912240
ISBN-13: 978-1-47929-408-4
ISBN-10: 147929408X
BISAC: Human Sexuality/Codes of Behavior/Politics of Morality

Printed in the USA

Also by the Author:

"Memories and Lessons
 of my young life in Wartime Germany"

"The Phases of Our Lives"

IN SEARCH

OF A

NEW MORALITY

Essays

On Love, Sex And Politics
In Our Modern World

Wolfgang Mack PhD
Second Edition 2016

In Search of a New Morality

The Essays:

Acknowledgement

In putting together my thoughts on Morality I had the good fortune of invaluable inputs from friends and from my family on their own thoughts on Morality in our modern world. I owe all of them many thanks for their constructive contributions to help me present credible views on this most important subject.

And I owe a very special "Thank You" to my lovely wife Francesca for her tireless editing and for her many improvements of these Essays. Without our son Christoph's help to lead me into the electronic age I could not have managed to get this book done.

I sincerely hope that my readers may find these Essays not only informative but also helpful to evaluate the many divergent views that compete for our attention in the current discourse on what is moral, and what is not, in our personal and in our public lives.

Foreword

- Why do some societies have different moral principles, but which ones are valid for everyone?

- Why is it so difficult for our 'faith-based' and for 'progressive' groups to agree on public policies regarding personal moral choices?

- Why have the rules on our sexual behavior changed so much in the last few generation ?

- And why are we getting so worked up over occasional sexual missteps by people in power when we should pay a lot more attention to the Morality of their decision making?

These are some of the questions about the real meaning of Morality in the context of our own times.

Morality tells us what's right and wrong, and how to balance our own wants and desires with the needs and the interests of others. Morality is all-encompassing - it is the foundation for the laws we give ourselves to regulate our behavior in our personal lives, in politics, in the government we establish, and even for our conduct in wars. We cannot separate one sphere of Morality from another. They all intertwine, but obviously for us as individuals how we behave in our sexual lives is of very great and immediate importance to us. It is certainly one of the biggest issues in our lives, greatly influencing what kind of person we are.

But that is just one of the many areas of our human existence where it is necessary to have basic rules of behavior, a standard that establishes what is morally acceptable and what is not. We need those standards also in our institutions, in our schools, and especially in our government. All too often we are strangely fixated on the personal moral issues in our private lives when we should give a lot more attention to moral deficits in these other areas. Prosecutions, wars and oppression come about not because of imperfections in our private lives but because of Immorality in the public arena- that is where we need to watch out for signs of Immorality that can be fatal for our society.

To what extent should 'government' or our religious institutions be allowed to tell us what is moral and what is not in our private lives? Historically speaking, both the earthly powers and religious organizations do have a very sorry record whenever they have imposed their own rigid concepts of Morality. Are they now any better at telling us what is moral than in the past?

In the past, organized religions assumed the role of guardians of public and personal Morality. In most modern societies the wisdom and effectiveness of this traditional set-up is being hotly being discussed considering its very controversial history. Even today extreme religions are playing a very destructive role in the personal and public lives of their nations. Against this disastrous historic background should we follow faith-based teachings about Morality? Where else should we look for guidance? Would we better off to use our own faculty of reasoning? Should we even make laws to dictate moral behavior? The present discourse on these fundamental questions is a very difficult one because by definition the faith-based camp view facts are subordinate to their beliefs, and the progressives do not really know how to deal with the depth of convictions of the faith-based camp.

In the end, our moral judgements should always be based on the realities of what is really going on in the life around us, not just on what we may wish them to be. This is especially important when we are confronted with moral standards in other cultures that are very different from ours. We cringe when we see grown men in some countries forcing pre-puberty girls into marriage, the same men who consider it a crime worth killing if these girls would show their faces in public.

But let's be humble: many of us may see the moral codes of other cultures as unreasonable or oppressive, but future generations may well look back at our own present day moral codes as incomprehensible and even absurd. Just look at what was 'moral' not so long ago in our very own history, like slavery and hanging 'witches'. Remember that it is always easy for those living in the present to feel superior to those who have lived in the past, or in what we sometimes call 'backward societies'. Obviously moral standards do indeed vary very much in different parts of our world, and if we want to make progress in living with these differences we must remain open for discussion. Shutting off rational examination will inevitably lead to the type of medieval repression that the modern western world has largely overcome but is very much alive in some ideologically controlled societies.

No matter how we deal with these issues, living a moral life matters. It makes us human and makes our lives a lot more meaningful. Governments, too, can not succeed in the long run when they do not act morally.

In Search of a New Morality

Worried About The Decline In Morality?

From a report about another scandal hitting the Senate:

In yesterday's tumultuous session the senior senator rose to his feet, angrily demanding the floor. Still cutting a commanding figure he has earned the respect of his peers for his statesmanship and his unrelenting fight against corruption, but in doing so he has also made himself hated by those whose lies and misdeeds he had exposed in the past. Now he was visibly shaken: the Senate had just acquitted a fellow Senator from a charge of bribery to secure high government offices for some clearly unworthy influence peddlers. Bribery has always been considered a really serious offense in the Senate, deserving punishment or at least censure - it was going against all the fine traditions of his party. This bribery affair was especially damaging having trumpeted the party's claim for their high standards on moral values and respect for the law. It now made them look like a bunch of hypocrites. "What ever happened to our time-honored values, our sense of decency, our morals?" the old senator shouted at the hushed chamber.

But his experience with twenty years of the Senate's convoluted workings should have taught him to watch more carefully for cues from his peers, and especially from his opponents. What he apparently did not see yesterday was that he may be losing this battle. His political career may be about to evaporate - too many enemies in both parties from too many past fights. He slowly made his way back and with a sigh of resignation slumped into his seat.

"O tempera, O mores!"

That was his outcry about his disdain for what he saw as the changing moral environment in his days. The year was 58 BCE, and the senator's name was Marcus Tullius Cicero: patriot, orator and fearless leader in Rome's republican days. He was openly attacking corruption, and especially those who had used their wealth for shamelessly buying their way into the highest offices.

We don't know very much about the details of the actual happenings, but Cicero's life story is definitely true. As he foresaw, he would be exiled and eventually murdered a few years later by those who had once too often been found with their hands in the public treasury.

When people today quote his famous "Oh tempera, Oh mores" they invariably use it to address what they believe to be the decline of *sexual* Morality. Cicero, like many upright Romans in Rome's golden era was indeed a defender of personal Virtue and what he saw as a loosening of sexual mores was certainly a part of his worries.

However, that was not the at center of his concerns. From all the surviving records of Cicero's timeless Senate speeches it is clear that he was mainly addressing the changing attitudes of what was honorable, and therefore considered 'moral', in government, business and, above all, in politics. That was where he saw the moral decay in his days - corruption in government, the poorly concealed bribing of politicians and the rigging of regulations to benefit insiders. Those were the changes he was afraid of, and those he fought un-compromisingly, regardless of the dangers to himself. He understood very well that the deterioration of basic morals in government and politic would cut the very root of justice and liberty which had been the pride of Rome's Republic and the envy of people all over the ancient world. Just as he had predicted, the growing immorality in government and politics would soon cause Rome to slide back into tyranny by demented dictators.

It simply shows that changes in moral codes, good or bad, are nothing new, that has been going on for a long time. It's just that in our modern world changes in our personal moral standards seem to have come so rapidly that it has been hard for some of us to keep up with them. So many of us still long for the past's perceived tranquility, the 'good old days', when moral choices seemed clear-cut, a matter of 'black and white'. But under that mask of assuredness of our previous generations' morals the same hormones were raging in all humans, the same yearning for power and domination, and the same greed for possessions as we are experiencing them now. In their times they were exposed to the same temptations that face us today and they often succumbed to them just as we do now.

None of that has changed. What has changed is that we are able and willing to be more open to talk about moral issues. It is not that we have become better or worse than our ancestors, rather we had to adjust our concept of morals to reflect the changing circumstances of our lives in our time, whether we like it or not.

No generation is ever comfortable with changing moral standards. Perhaps life would be easier without the uncertainties of change. But this would not be reality. *Change is the only constant in our lives.*

Inevitable, however, changes in moral codes have consequences. In politics and government, a decline in Morality will result in loss of liberty and justice. Changes in sexual Morality change the way we look at marriage, and it affects civility in everyday relationships. The question is how we should cope with a changing world, and *which* changes we are willing to accept.

But only as long as we can have open and constructive discussions about moral issues do we stand a chance that our personal and public lives can be lived in peace and liberty.

Where does today's Morality come from?

Moral decisions are effective only when based on a core of shared values that are accepted as sensible and constructive. But how are we to decide which rules about Morality are valid and which are not? Where do our present day rules come from and why are some of them different from those in our venerated traditional texts?

Is there a set of moral codes innate in all human beings that would be valid uniformly for all people and for all times, an *absolute*? Or is Morality subject to change in accordance with the prevailing needs of societies, a *relative*?

It's not as simple as some people may wish it to be - some moral codes are absolute, and some are not. There are some basic moral rules that are indeed unchangeable and valid for all humans at all times. They are listed unambiguously in those parts of our timeless Commandments that deal with what's essential for living in a community:

- *Honor your parents,*
- *Do not kill,*
- *Do not lie,*
- *Do not steal*
- *and do not commit adultery.*

Many religions have framed these common-sense, socially oriented Commandments as divinely inspired, and many of us find comfort in the thought that in this way their authority is put beyond question. And they should be: There is no society in the world that can exist without these ground rules. We should be grateful for our religious institutions that have been the guardians of these basic societal rules of moral behavior through the ages. They are - and always will be - the foundation for any human society to function as a community. In this sense, they are indeed an "absolute".

In parallel with the establishing of our Commandments came the recognition that there also is a need for quite specific rules what *not* to do in our personal lives, to make sure that we humans do not destroy ourselves with from within with bad habits. These very personal vices are known as the "Seven Deadly Sins": Lust, Gluttony, Greed, Sloth, Anger, Envy and Pride. In Antiquity, avoiding these vices was considered the highest human achievement: the *Virtuous* life. On the surface, the Seven Deadly Sins are there, first and foremost, for our own protection, to keep us healthy physically and mentally. In the end, however, committing any one of the Seven Deadly Sins also will damage societal living, as habitual violation of these rules will undermine trust, and the sinners will eventually become a burden to others after having ruined their health. Following this reasoning, we may just as well add one more deadly sin of our modern age, the Eighth: Over-Indulgence in alcohol, tobacco or drugs, which will eventually destroy a person's health and mind, eventually to become a burden to society, just like the original Seven.

Together, these basic rules have defined human Morality throughout the ages. However, even with the clear knowledge of the beneficial effect of the Commandments for the community, and the warning about the Seven Deadly Sins for our own welfare, the sad fact remains that there were too many abuses and misinterpretations leading to some old 'moral' practices that had to be changed as our life circumstances changed - we no longer are the biblical herdsmen, the medieval hunters or the Arab nomads. Most of us now live in highly organized communities and depend on man-made laws and a lot of technology for our survival. All of this is vastly different from the conditions of those of our ancestors who had developed 'moral' codes commensurate with the way they lived. Inevitably new rules of behavior became necessary as life styles changed. These then are the moral rules that are "relative".

For those of us who like to look to our venerated religious texts for guidance on all moral issues it is important to understand that some of the traditional moral codes established there prescribe human behavior as it was *necessary* and *practical* for securing the well-being of the community *under the life circumstances of their days,* with penalties for not following the then prevailing rules of behavior (committing a sin) commensurate with the way they lived and in keeping with the customs of their times. Their rules of conduct - their moral codes - were obviously right for them and necessary for their survival, but some of them are no longer appropriate to our times.

For example, these ancient texts forbade adultery because they knew that the stability of the family would be threatened, and thus the coherence of their communities. Certainly, this is still of very much a concern to us now. Similarly, they were strictly forbidding incest, based on their very sensible observation that inbreeding would result in birth defects with its detrimental consequences for family and community. This was also effective and necessary for the protection of next of kin from sexual exploitation within the family. All this is still valid, but in our modern world we no longer stone the perpetrators to death.

When they made women's virginity a condition for marriage, it was a very practical way to combat sexually transmitted diseases and to avoid unwanted pregnancies. These are still valid concerns today, but at least in the modern Western world, we no longer kill those who have lost their virginity before marriage.

Likewise, the almost paranoid condemnation of homosexuality in these texts was probably caused more by concerns that it might diminish the size and power of the tribe than by moral objections alone. It is noteworthy that this also shows that homosexuality, male and female - as well as bisexuality - have been around at least for the recorded history and most likely in the same proportions to the rest of the population as now. Whatever the old reactions to these facts were, in the modern world most of us no longer consider them as moral issues but as the result of natural dispositions. But mindlessly perpetuating these ancient attitudes have haunted humanity for centuries and still persist even in a part of our modern world.

For many of us it is a sobering fact that rules on human behavior - moral codes - do change with time. What was accepted as moral at one time in history quite often would be considered highly immoral just a few generations later:

- ‣ When the Inquisition tortured their victims it most likely never occurred to the torturers that what they did to 'save their souls' would be regarded as hugely immoral two hundred years later.

- ‣ And the spiritual powers not so long ago saw nothing immoral in burning people at the stake if they would not accept the dogmas of their times (such as the Earth being the center of the universe). Similarly, when our Puritan forefathers were hanging 'witches' they most likely were totally convinced that they were entirely moral in doing so.

▸ Even the practice of human sacrifices in biblical times, or by cultures like the pre-Columbian Indians, was obviously not considered immoral by them at but most certainly is now.

▸ In our own days we are not immune to the scourge of practicing torture, often sanctioned by states or religions, with not enough of an outcry about its gross Immorality.

▸ And until quite recently in our very own country the most abject racial discrimination, even slavery, was the norm, sanctioned and enforced by law and widely practiced even in our churches, with little thought given to its enormous Immorality.

From today's vantage point we are horrified by all these atrocities but we should not rush to judgement of the historic persons who committed these acts. In their times, and under the conditions of their lives in their society they must have believed that what they were doing was right and therefore moral - *their confusing sets of irrational beliefs were at fault.* We cannot simply say that they were bad people and condemning them for their deeds would be missing the point - *our present moral codes simply are different from theirs.*

This leaves us with the question about what the rules of moral behavior really should be in our modern world. Which of the 'traditional' values are we to keep and which of the new rules should apply in our lives? Are we to look to our churches, our institutions or our government to tell us what is moral or not, or is it the personal responsibility of each one of us to find a set of moral guidelines that make us comfortable within ourselves and safe in the communities in which we live?

In our modern world, the all-important issue is that any responsible person, or institution, must allow free inquiry into questions of all human behavior, personal or public. Whatever our political or religious persuasions we must remain on guard that we do not fall back into the the type of mind set of intolerance that led the Athenians kill their Socrates, just because he asked questions that some of them found too probing for their comfort.

Not interested in stuff that happened in the very distant past? How about much more recent governments like Hitler's Germany, Pinochet's Chile, Stalin's Russia - these were places where politicians took it upon themselves to tell their people what was moral and what was not - and just look at the disasters they created by imposing their particular world view on their citizens. Obviously we do not want this type of moral coercion in our modern world. But if we choose to take responsibility for our own personal moral choices, will that leave us without any guidance? And how can we leave it to everyone to make up their own rules? Would that not lead to utter chaos, with everyone going in different directions?

Not if we follow the most universal of all moral codes, the time-honored "Golden Rule":

Do onto others as you would have them do unto you.

This is the most fundamental and universal statement about Morality that can serve as a test to check every law, every dogma, every political program for its moral value, independent of any bias or personal belief. It is as infallible as anything can be in this world, a truly reliable litmus test for our personal and public Morality.

Is Morality all about Sex?

For her it had been a difficult day. At the office she had to clean up some paperwork before getting into her car heading home. She was running late, and weekend traffic was slow. She picked up her cellphone telling the babysitter that she would be late coming home. Then she saw the big SUV coming at her from the side street.

For him it had been a very good day. His big contract had finally come through. Happy partners, lots of back-slapping and toasting to their success. Couldn't wait to go home to give his wife the good news. Trying to make the intersection as the light was changing he ran into that car.

At first the accident looked like a typical evening rush hour mishap, his SUV broad-siding her minivan. Nobody was hurt, but both cars were a mess. Stunned, she still was holding on to her cell phone in total disbelief as he was yelling at her "why could you not watch where you were going instead of gabbing on your d**** phone..." But had she not seen him running the red light, much too fast for her to get out of his way?

Several policemen were trying to clear the intersection to let traffic moving again. One policeman was asking for eye witnesses: yes, the SUV had been running the red light. To the SUV driver: please get out of the car. Did the policeman smell something on the man's breath? But the man took the policeman aside: look, don't do anything foolish here, mind your career, I know the mayor and I could call your chief.

The policeman turned his attention to her. He pulled out his citation book. She was a very attractive woman and he could not resist the temptation: "Maybe the two of us could get together and if you treat me right, you know, I may forget this whole thing....". She understood perfectly well - a little sex would avoid all the problems that come with a citation, the trouble with her car insurance and the precedents for future infractions. No way, she said and "besides the baby sitter is still on the line and heard you". That scared the policeman. He could lose his job for soliciting sex.

So his report said "the cause of the accident could not be determined with certainty". But how about the guy who had witnessed it? Had he not left his address with the policeman? Somehow nothing further was done.

Here you have a host of legal issues - false testimony, falsifying official documents, influence peddling, overt or hidden sexual or racial bias, open or implied blackmail. Each one is also a moral matter. Do all these moral issues carry the same weight, or are there different levels of importance?

Now let's do a little quiz: in the above case which of all these moral offenses do you consider the most serious? Which do you see as the most or the least damaging to the persons involved, or to society, to public safety or to our justice system? Do not say they are all equally serious - try to give your honest opinion about their ranking.

If you have put the policeman's sexist advances at the top of your list of moral seriousness you are probably with the majority. In media reports on cases like this, 'sexual harassment' will steal just about all the headlines with scant attention given to the other moral transgressions. Strange: while in some respects we have become much freer in sexual matters we also have become so much more squeamish about even the slightest innuendo of sexual misconduct. But after sober reflection could you not conclude that those other moral violations are a lot more serious? Would they not have a much greater effect on the individuals involved or on the community?

Clearly in the above example the policeman's sexist advances were unacceptable and certainly hurtful, but would destroying that man's livelihood be a *moral equivalent* of that transgression? Are the other moral failures in this story not equal or in the end even more serious offenses to society's interests?

Still, whenever the subject of Morality comes up it is mostly the sexual issues that seem to get all the attention. The reasons for this are not that difficult to see. We have to make decisions on our own private behavior all the time and we are expected to exert some level of control over it. By contrast, public moral issues are largely outside our personal control and with only a distant possibility of influencing them, and then only indirectly, such as at voting time. Too many of us conclude therefore that it is useless to try to do something about Immorality in the public policy sphere.

There are plenty of examples where our fixation on the sexual aspects of Morality is drowning out our concerns about moral failings in the politics of our communities and our nation. But colossal moral failures are at the root of social injustice, the manipulations of financial markets, wars, persecutions and poverty, each one causing infinitely more misery for the human race than all the sexual trespasses in the world.

How did it happen that we have become so totally absorbed by even the most trivial cases of sexual misbehavior, and why are we ready to quickly elevate them beyond proportion into hugely exaggerated indignation? Have we all become neurotics, innerly afraid of anything very personal? All this while we tolerate even the most flagrant Immorality in so many of our public policy decisions, more or less shrugging off corruption and greed and letting politicians buy their positions of power with money and 'favors'.

Of course, persons in the public eye, especially our policy makers, are expected to be held to a 'higher standard'. But that 'higher standard' should first of all be applied to the quality of the work that we expect from them, their dedication to keep us safe and to better our lives. Their personal habits are a private matter and they have to account for their shortcomings only to themselves and their families, just as everybody else.

But how can we trust them in their official functions as policy makers if they are not even able or willing to control their primal bodily urges? There may be some good reason to put this into question. However, let us first look at their effectiveness in doing the work they are hired to do before we condemn them for their personal habits.

Quite a few politicians and public figures are keenly aware of our natural bias, knowing full well that sex-related matters will captivate the attention of many segments of our population much more readily than potentially lethal moral failures in the public sphere. Exploiting our perennial preoccupation with sex can easily get in the way of much needed discussions on pressing social and economic problems. After all, sex scandals are easy for the public to talk about but it is a lot more demanding for the public's attention to deal with the more complex issues of Morality in politics, in our legal system, and whether public funds are well guarded or not.

In the past our teachings about Morality were essentially about how to conduct ourselves in our very personal sphere. Now our discussions on Morality must concern itself at least equally with how our public affairs are managed, how we are governed. Take for example the "Citizens United" decision of our Supreme Court lifting the last limitations corporate financial contributions, even for *foreigners,* creating the opportunity for unlimited and utterly shameless programs of overt bribery of our lawmakers. Our Founding Fathers would find this an intolerable travesty - had they not risked life and fortune to free us from foreign domination?

The moral quality of the our public policy making will determine how we deal with the real problems like poverty, the inequities of our educational systems and our uneven efforts to protect our environment from being ravaged. These are the issues that will determine the future quality of life for us and our descendants and the security of our communities, our Nation. Morality in our personal lives is a precondition for our own emotional stability. Morality in our public policy making is essential for peace and prosperity. Both are necessary. Neglecting any one of them may endanger our safety and even our human existence.

In Search of a New Morality

What is personal Morality, really?

In a deep South private high school for boys a sixteen year old had sex with a fifteen year old girl from a neighboring school for girls. Inspired by the movie "American Beauty", the boy had videotaped their tryst and the next day showed it to his lacrosse teammates. None of them objected or asked for the video to be stopped. A day or two later the school's headmaster learned about the tape and so did the girl's mother.

The headmaster and the girl's mother were, of course, in turmoil - the mother furious about her daughter's humiliation, the headmaster fearing damaging publicity for him and his school which prided itself of the highest ethical standards, requiring among many other religious devotions a daily chapel attendance for their students.

So far, the matter had not been made public. No legal charges had been made. Their sex had been consensual. To do nothing was definitely an option for both the headmaster and the mother. All could soon be forgotten like so many other youthful indiscretions. They could decide to bury the matter and avoid uncomfortable questions about the headmaster's competence, or the youngsters' reputation, and above all, the lacrosse team's championship status. But would it be doing the morally right thing?

After almost two weeks of soul-searching the headmaster decided to open the issue head-on, putting his own position at risk by calling a meeting with parents, school trustees and the lacrosse team and said this:

"I am expelling the boy for humiliating his girlfriend by making this video and then showing it to his schoolmates, I suspend those students who participated in the girl's humiliation, and as punishment of the lacrosse players for not having stood up to protect the girl I am canceling the remaining lacrosse season." He added "I know that this is dealing a devastating blow to your hopes for a championship, but you will have to recognize that you have crossed the line by your failure in common morality."

Was it all about two young people having sex? Note that it was not that his 16 year old student had sex with a 15 year old girl that was at the center of the headmaster's judgement - not that he approved of such relationships in his school or anywhere else. But no matter how much he might disapprove, their sex had been consensual *and thus there was no personal harm done at that point.* What the headmaster saw as the much more serious offense was the videotaping that the boy had done without telling the girl. That was not consensual and thus *immoral.* Then, by showing his video to his team mates he publicly embarrassed the girl *and thus caused actual harm.* On top of this offense came the deplorable lack of moral sense of his team mates for not making him stop the video and thus inflicting *additional harm* to the girl by their passive complicity.

This was big. The headmaster could quite easily have stuck to the conventional reaction that for his students to have sex would be the central issue. But he rightly saw the much bigger problem in his students' failure to do the morally right thing in protecting the dignity of the girl, starting with the boy making the video and to have shown it to others who then failed to stop it. That is where *harm* was done and where the real issue of Morality came in. When harm is done we need to take corrective action and mete out punishment when indicated. But merely having offended the personal moral sensitivities of bystanders does not justify rebuke or punishment - that would be assuming the right of non-participants to morally judge others. Only when *real harm* is done there is reason to invoke moral rules. Just the belief alone that some one's personal sensitivities might be offended, or that some one's rules of behavior might have been violated does not justify moral censor. It is only real harm that gives rise to intervention.

In the end it was the headmaster's courage to concentrate on what he saw as the really important moral aspect of the case that earned him the respect from everyone. Even the lacrosse team understood - and accepted - their hard lesson. Had it not been for the headmaster's wisdom and measured decision, this sensitive matter could have gone quite easily in a very different direction with much anger and resentment and without really addressing the underlying moral significance of the issue. In the midst of pressures he found an ethically motivated decision that avoided the temptations of so many extreme 'right-versus-wrong' mind-sets that mostly would lead to nothing but moral dead ends.

Some bystanders made it a point that instead of leaving it to the judgement of the educator, the state should have stepped in and apply its laws for the protection of minors. Would the outcome have been any better?

In matters of Morality, there is no substitute for personal responsibility and common sense, still the best guarantee for sensible solutions of moral issues. It always leads to confusion, and often to unwarranted complications whenever the state - or any public institution - tries to force their views on the personal judgement of thoughtful individuals.

No government program can ever be a valid substitute for personal responsibility and common decency.

It's not only the Big Issues that matter.

High school was a breeze for MarieLouise. Popular, athletic and smart, she got good grades even in her less favorite classes like math and chemistry. She was confident to ace the up-coming college admissions tests - except for failing French. Somehow she just had not put enough effort into it and was afraid now that she would blow her chances for getting into the college of her choice.

Her parents could not understand. After all they were originally French and had come to this country from Vietnam - her father had been a translator for the US Armed forces. When the war ended he had fled Vietnam and with the help of the Army moved to the US. MarieLouise grew up as the 'All-American Girl' and as it happens so often with the sons and daughters of immigrants she wanted to speak only English, wanting to be 'just like everybody else'.

Now the chips were down. Tears were flowing. Was it too late? Sobbing turned to anger, to recrimination and the inevitable 'I told you so...'

And then MarieLouise had an idea: Mom, you look just like me, you have the same name, you are fluent in French, and the make-up test will be out of town, far from people who know us - why don't you just sit in for me - there are over a hundred others taking the test, no one will notice.

After some soul-searching they concluded that it was really not such a bad thing, and they did it. Her Mom's fluency in French would get her daughter the grades she needed. The college of her choice would be within grasp.

All through their lives her Mom and Dad had been very principled people - following the strict moral codes of their days. They were married very young and had their only child a little more than a year after. Still quite young looking, Mom could indeed easily step in for her daughter and most probably would not be found out. The primal parental urge to do everything to protect their daughter won over their hesitations and doubts. Getting into the exam room unchallenged, acing the test and getting MarieLouise into her college were the easy parts.

But aside from the issue of legality, had they done the *morally* right thing? Was it worth the self-doubt to come, their conscience gnawing at their inner peace, their growing understanding that they had abandoned the values of their up-bringing? How would they live with the knowledge that by cheating they may have destroyed a chance for another possibly more deserving student? How do you deal with the corrosive problem of guilt?

All these are good reasons why following your own sense of Morality is a good thing - it is of invaluable help to prevent you from falling for the temptation to do wrong when you think it is convenient. But the real damage resulting from this type of cheating is done to the very person we think we have helped. Why? Surely, cheating may get you where you otherwise would not be or do not deserve to be, but how much good did it do for MarieLouise to get into a school where among other things she would be expected to perform well in French, when in reality she was not interested enough to do the hard work needed to master the language? And what would it do to her self-respect, her ability in the future to deal with difficult situations on her own, with no parent around to bail her out?

It is not just in the big issues of life where difficult moral decisions have to be made - it is in the many small issues of our very day lives when we need to follow our inner *moral compass.*

This is especially true because decisions on moral issues are rarely made in a clear-cut set of circumstances. Usually there are many sides to be considered - let's be careful before we rush to judgement. For example, social conditions have a great bearing on what is moral and what is not. It is easy to be 'good' when your basic needs are met - food, shelter, personal safety and bodily health. But sometimes these conditions are not met - stealing food for greed is one thing, stealing for your and your family's *survival* is morally speaking quite a different matter.

In his "Three Penny Opera", Bert Brecht's scathing criticism of social injustice, he makes his beleaguered protagonist shout out in rage at the moralizing world around him:

"First give us something to eat, then you can talk to us about your Morality!"

The true quality of our moral convictions shows in our action when there is trouble and when things are not quite as clear as we would wish them to be. Those who enjoy the comfort of feeling absolutely sure of the validity of their own Morality should be reminded that whenever any of us has this agreeable sensation of being impressibly moral, *we may not be moral at all.* There may be some very undesirable character deficiencies lurking underneath, such as self-righteousness which many consider the exact opposite of Morality.

Why Our Sex Mores Were Bound To Change

In our modern world we are much freer to enjoy our sexual lives than ever before but what does that tell us about our Morality? How should we morally judge the fact that just about all our young people are sexually active at an early age and that sex before marriage is now pretty much taken for granted in many circles? Why did these attitudes change so much in the past few generations, and why did they become a new reality so fast?

It happened because our *life circumstances changed,* and they changed in big ways. The biggest single change was the phenomenal increase in life expectancy caused in turn by the advances in science and medicine, and out of this came significant changes in our personal behavior:

▸ *We marry much later in life.*

In the times when our old sexual codes were established most people would get married in their 'teens'. It was quite reasonable then to demand that these young people should not have sex until married. Today, at that age, most of our youngsters are still in high school, and getting established in a trade or profession takes many more years of preparation than in the past. As a result most of us are getting married much later, often in their thirties. How can we realistically expect our young people to go without sex for more than ten of their their most vibrant years? No matter how hard one may try, this just would not be realistic. No wonder that the moral codes governing youthful behavior were to change.

▸ *We live a lot longer.*

Not so long ago the average life expectancy in Western countries (for those who made it through childhood) was not much more than 35 years for men and about 32 years for women. Average life expectancy in modern societies is now well above 80 years, often in relatively good health compared with previous generations. This means in effect that people now can be intimate for about three times as many years in their life time. In such a long life couples may grow closer to each other, reaching a happy state of emotional and spiritual contentment - that is the good outcome. Or, they may grow apart - that is one of the main causes for the growing rate of divorce, often leading to multiple sequential marriages. As much as we may dislike it, divorce has become wide-spread, and not necessarily because people have lower morals.

▸ *More unmarried couples are living together.*

About one third of all people in their twenties do, according to Dr. Meg Jay, Clinical Psychologist at the University of Virginia. Jay draws mixed conclusions on this development. On the positive side, living together before getting married certainly helps to get to know each other intimately. This is how you find out how sensitive your partner is to your feelings and to your physical needs. You will see a lot of the other's way of living, from his world view, his hang-ups all the way to whether he will flush the toilet.

You think all this is superficial? It is better to discover bad habits, character flaws and about issues of physical compatibility before making a life-long commitment. However, when done without much thought given to a longer-term commitment or when done just for convenience or economic necessity, such co-habitation has its own problems, as it is easy to slip into it and much more difficult to exit. Also, co-habitation tends to prevent young people from getting to know others to augment their circle of friends and finding other potential future marriage prospects - they are giving up too much of their freedoms. The same can be said about the idea of 'going steady' that was the accepted moral rule for high school-age youngsters a few decades ago.

▸ *We live in different environments.*

Only a few generations ago over 80% of all people lived in the countryside, on isolated farms or in small towns where most knew each other. Now the reverse is the case. In the modern world almost 85% are living in cities, with much higher social mobility and much greater chances of making new contacts at work, in social gatherings and in travel. It has become a lot easier to enter into new personal relationships.

▸ *Advances in birth control in effect weakened the connection between having sex and pregnancy.*

Not having to fear unintended pregnancy puts decisions of whether to have sex or not squarely into the arena of moral choice and not so much dictated by fear. Justly many believe that decisions made purely on moral grounds are spiritually much superior to those made out of fear of the consequences.

It is by these changes in our life circumstances that the changes in sexual norms have become inevitable. No government program, no religious dogma, no well-meaning preaching about 'abstinence' can change this. These are facts, and it is largely immaterial whether one likes them or not. In no way should we equate these changes with lack of good morals - it is our life circumstances that caused the changes.

We should not waste our energies in a futile attempt to 'stem the tide', but neither should we just leave it to the peer pressures that our youngsters are subject to, or to the 'gurus' out there who are pushing their own agendas. And we should not give up hope that parents will put their values about responsibility into the upbringing of their children.

Trying to counteract these changes with ill-advised government programs or faith-based initiatives will lead only to confusion. Politics cannot change the underlying fundamentals.

Sometimes Morals must adjust to sustain Life

"Those who are the most moral
  are usually the ones that are the furthest from the problem."
  (Saul Alinski, American humanistic activist,1909-1972)

Sitting across from their Perce Nez hosts in the Chieftain's wigwam Second Lieutenant William Clark looked questioningly at Captain Lewis. They had been rescued from certain starvation by these Indians and were grateful for their hospitality and for their help to get the expedition back on track. But their faithful travel companion Sacajawea had just translated the strangest proposal from the Chief -

he had just requested that before leaving Lewis should impregnate one of his daughters. Lewis thought he had not heard right - how can a father openly offer his daughter to a stranger who was about to leave them? Was this a trap, or was he being tested, but for what? The Chief saw that Lewis was confused. Patiently the Chief explained that among the leaders in his tribal world it was customary that they

would 'sire' a child with one of the other leaders' daughters using the off-spring as a sort of hostage to ensure friendly and durable relations. Neither Lewis nor Clark knew what to make of this situation until Sacajawea whispered in Lewis' ear that turning down the Chief's request would be a capital offense that could lead to an immediate massacre. There was no way to out.

Lewis would indeed father a son with the Chief's daughter. He eventually came to live with Lewis after the successful end of the historic expedition (according to Dr. Jay Buckley, History Professor at Brigham University). You don't often read about this part because it obviously does not fit into the image of our standard American Morality, but from the perspective of the Indians and the explorers it made a lot of good sense. In fact for the expedition's survival it was probably even unavoidable and thus morally right *under its circumstances.* And compared with the many atrocious acts committed by us against our Native Americans you could even say that their moral code actually speaks of a much better humanity than the White Man's.

What is moral and what is not is determined ultimately by the necessities of life, with codes of behavior following those needs. There are plenty of case histories about how Morality is inevitably molded by the needs of specific circumstances.

Many of us still look to the Bible and other ancient texts as venerated moral guides with their great stories about history, their portrayals of extraordinary men and women, and their uplifting poetry. Many of the Bible's teachings about Morality undoubtedly were very much in sync with the way people lived at that time. However, some of them are hardly acceptable for us now.

For example, in Biblical times slavery was practiced in most parts of the world, and women were considered chattel. Having multiple wives was quite the norm, in fact encouraged, certainly for the economically successful - they were the ones who could afford it. In their times this made some sense - most likely there were more women than marriageable men because of wars and slavery. Disobedient sons would be killed and conquered tribes were sold into slavery. In the conditions under which people lived in biblical times these rules probably made sense and therefore were 'moral'. Because our lives are different now many of those practices simply no longer are acceptable.

But the Bible is not the only place that shows us how life circumstances determine the way we humans deal with matters of moral behavior.

Consider the mating habits in very small communities living in isolated and very difficult-to-reach places, like small islands, or in very remote mountains - there, visiting males from other areas are often invited to mate with the local women. Refusing to do so would be considered a grave insult. Marco Polo scandalized his world when he reported these observations from his travels through desolate parts of Central Asia. Later there were plenty of similar reports from early explorers of small Pacific islands.

But even now some of these habits exist in some parts of the world. In her in-depth study of life in the present-day Arctic, the renowned journalist Sara Wheeler reports that 'loaning out wives' is a widely recognized practice among the arctic natives who live in small isolated communities far from the nearest major settlements.

Another example of other groups' moral codes is the well documented (and often erroneously deplored) habit of small nomadic tribes to steal or trade other tribes' women back and forth. This was not just done maliciously - it was a matter of long-term survival by enlarging their genetic pool. The tribes that did not do this or did not have the necessary bargaining power would fail to get new blood into their small bands and eventually would simply cease to exist.

Why do these habits seem immoral to so many of us? They were not immoral to the people living under these conditions. Their real life experience had taught them, over time, that they always needed new bloodlines to avoid inbreeding which would threaten their genetic health. In the long run they could not have survived otherwise. With all our modern understanding of genetics this should not be shocking to us. It was in fact a very wise and unavoidable measure to ensure survival.

Our anthropologists tell us that nomadic tribes had no concept of private property. This is not just the speculation of researchers - we saw that in those of our own North American Indian tribes who were still 'hunters and gatherers' when our forefathers pushed their way into their territories. These nomadic Indian tribes were sharing whatever little they had, and more often than not this would include their mates. To them it did not matter who were the fathers and the mothers of the children - the entire tribe would take responsibility for their well-being. Having as many mates as possible was necessary to assure the diversity of genes needed for healthy propagation, and this moral code served them well in the realities of their lives.

Our Northwest Indians were different. According to Vine Deloria, these tribes' foremost chronicler, they were already living in settled communities and thus had developed a keen sense of personal property and lived in monogamous families. Still, their land was not owned by anyone, and they were totally perplexed by the white man's obsession with the idea of land ownership. But curiously these Northwest natives had a keen sense of 'property' when it came to their fishing rights, marking off specific whale hunting reserves for each tribe,.

Monogamy as we know it today became the social norm only when people began to live in permanent settlements where they had the ability to accumulate property. When it was time to pass the family property or social position on to the next generation it became important to know who had fathered the prospective heir - hence the need for monogamous mating relationships that are now our moral code. For some societies, like those in biblical times and even today in some backward countries, this did not preclude a man having multiple wives - the important thing was to know who the father was.

Those who think the habits of these societies are a bit too lurid for our taste need to be reminded that the people who lived under these particular circumstances had nothing tantalizing in mind - they just lived their lives as they had to. It was the only way for their families to remain healthy and to survive, and for their communities to succeed in their geographically isolated places.

But then came the Western colonial powers with their missionaries in tow, determined to impose their own way of life on the hapless natives, with disastrous results. It was not only the venereal diseases and the smallpox that decimated the natives - seeing their time-honored values trampled upon broke their spirit. Abject poverty, rampant alcoholism and drug dependency were to follow. On top of their misery came a wave of birth defects and mental illnesses, mostly because of inbreeding, something they had previously avoided with their long established mating habits that were so offensive to the Western newcomers.

In their arrogance the colonial governments were determined to force their western morals upon those unsuspecting natives, not even bothering to find out why these natives had been living the way they did. Their set of morals had been useful for them, and the Western ones imposed on them by a misguided zeal to make them 'modern' just about destroyed them.

The 'moral' of this story: Governments with their politics are ill equipped to deal with Morality issues.

A Case For Better Sex Education

> *"Folks like us would never fuss*
> *With schools and books and learnin'*
> *Still we've gone from A to Z*
> *Doin' what comes naturally"*
> From Irvin Berlin's:"Annie, Get your Gun"

The battle for better sex education of our young people has a long history of misunderstandings and hypocrisy. Here are excerpts from some parents' interviews with their school's Counselors on their own experiences with sex education programs when they were young:

"Oh yes, I remember it well. I must have been 12 or 13. My little brother and I used to cringe when Mom and Pap would come back from their PTA meetings, all upset, occasionally whispering to each other trying not to let us know what the fuss was all about. But we knew - a battle royal was raging in our town about a proposal to introduce sex education in our school. We never were given the whole story. All we heard were words like 'preposterous' or 'have they no shame' and 'perverts'. I exchanged glances with my brother as he would roll his eyes, hoping not to get caught. "

"Our parents never talked to us about sex. Of course, we knew all about it, or at least we thought we did. How had we learned? Like all the other boys in school we found ways to sneak 'dirty' magazines

and we picked up some salacious gossip here and there, most of which in hindsight was very much off-the-mark. Well, our parents did make an effort - they would make appointments with our Pastor to 'inform' us. Listening to the nice man's wishy-washy platitudes we had to make a heroic effort not to snicker. Did it ever occur to him that he was making an utter fool of himself trying to connect with us while beating around the bush for an hour or so, giving us absolutely nothing of help. What he told us went about like this: "you are not to have sex of any kind until you will be married, and then it will be a sacred thing, and from now on don't talk about it any more."

"Well, we now have children of our own, two girls and a boy. We try to talk to them about sex but given our own conservative upbringing we are still a bit hesitant to tell them the full story. Whenever we start into it, all that our children tell us is that their sex education classes are just fine. Some parents had been bringing up fears that their children could be led into doing sex things just because they would have heard about them in class. We were all watching for tell-tale signs but did not see anything but fairly relaxed acceptance. At least now fewer parents are creating problems any more. So, what was all the fuss about in our days?"

By now formal sex education courses in schools and civic organizations are well established in most parts - hard to believe that until a generation or so ago this was generally considered *immoral.* It is also embraced by forward thinking faith-based groups, such as the Unitarian Universalist Association's curriculum "About your Sexuality" (later, in 1990, to merge with the United Church of Christ's "Our Whole Life" classes - OWL). Finally even these most conservative of institutions are coming around to develop programs to raise the level of responsibility in our young people for their most personal actions.

Their programs are based on the recognition that it is futile trying to keep youngsters in a state of innocence. One way or another our young ones will learn about the 'facts of life'. The question is what is the best and most constructive way to give them 'good' information that is realistic and factual, and to do it in a dignified, respectful and non-judgmental way. 'Moralizing', the opinionated preaching about how sexual morals *should* be, never works. Preaching 'abstinence' is a laudable effort but it mostly falls on deaf ears - it is an unrealistic expectation. It does nothing but heap more confusion and guilt upon our young ones.

After the 'non-judgmental' parts taught at our schools and institutions, the parents have to take over to fill in the 'judgmental' parts based on their own personal moral convictions. And let's not just talk about sex - talking in terms of "making love" sets a much better tone. And above all, let them know that there is a responsibility attached to all our our acts. Also, let's keep in mind that most teenagers simply are not ready to take this matter seriously enough. We need to be forthright in saying so directly and without ambiguity - they should wait until they are mature enough and are able and willing to live up to their responsibilities.

Tolerance for the life habits and preferences of others is an essential part of all these programs. Thankfully, a lot of progress has been made over the past decades in making our youngsters accept the fact that homosexuality and bisexuality are natural dispositions and not, as some moralists want you to believe, the result of a lack of 'good morals', and that everyone deserves our respect based solely on the quality of their character as a person.

But nothing less than open and factual information will do. As an example, read what Cardinal Timothy Dolan says in one of his personal blogs, lamenting the lack of clear information on such problems as pedophilia in his Church:

"Nothing in my own background or education equipped me to deal with this grave problem......no textbook or lecture ever referred to the sexual abuse of children."

This is what can happen if information is held back, even with persons we are looking to for moral guidance, and for setting examples.

Should we be concerned that freely available information and easy access to contraceptives will lead to more sexual activity? Maybe they will, especially for those who had abstained not because of moral considerations but because they were afraid of the potential consequences of pregnancy or STD. But not doing something out of fear of the consequences is morally speaking much inferior to the restraint based on an inner conviction when having sex is right and when it is not.

What is the right age to broach the subject of the 'facts of life' and how much sex talk is too much? No age is too early, as long as we answer their questions right on and not make a big deal of it beyond their level of understanding. No question is too direct to make us hold back on the facts. But let's keep questions and answers in perspective.

The little boy, after visiting the new neighbors who had just moved in asks his dad "Where did we come from?"

Ouch, thinks the father, here it comes, and he goes into a longwinded story about the birds and the bees and how moms get babies and all that.

The little boy, confused, looks at dad and says: "That's strange, our new neighbors came from Ohio...

The concept of being open, factual and full of real information is well represented in "The Marriage Bed", a Christian faith-based website. While primarily addressing married couples it is a valid resource for everyone who is interested in a sober and constructive study of today's sexual habits - they are discussed in such detail that would have been unthinkable in the past. And reputable institutions like the Guttmacher Institute are invaluable resources for any one who is seriously interested in knowing the reality of our younger people.

But what should we say to our young adults? Should we say nothing, leaving them to find their own way through the wildly differing ways of the world? They are being bombarded from all sides with 'life-style' messages which, like fads, come in and out of fashion with lightning speed, from 'abstinence' on one side and 'free love' on the other extreme of this very wide spectrum. However, mainstream books and op-pages on this delicate - and very difficult - subject offer many well reasoned suggestions that make sense and should become discussion points for conversations between mature people and youngsters. In the best case this what our young people hear:

There is no such thing as 'Free Love'. First of all, when that slogan was fashionable, it really meant 'free sex', with little regard for the emotional and spiritual welfare of the other person. The added statement "it's okay as long as you don't hurt somebody" is pretty self-serving, a cop-out. For one, when we have sex, it is not just the 'Other' that we need to be concerned for, but everybody we and the 'Other' know, their family, their friends, the community. And 'not to hurt somebody' (*a negative*) may show good intentions but is just not enough. What is needed is the intent and the ability to make sure that the outcome is a positive one - *for all around us*. And in all of this, let's not forget for both partners to have *fun*!

Making love is something very personal and it should not be done thoughtlessly. But it should also be understood that it is quite a natural thing to do. You will get the most out of love making when you *love* your partner - at least you should be good friends. Like in all relationships the over-arching criteria for being a good lover is *Decency* - it's as simple as that. And *Sincerity* is an essential part of it - *we cannot be moral without it*. Decency means being responsive to the needs and sensitivities of the '*Other*'. It means giving at least as much to the 'Other' as to yourself, even when passion tries to push your own needs into the fore. In a good relationship you must not take more than you give.

Being 'decent' is not the same as being 'modest'. The type of modesty that holds you back from creating and enjoying pleasure just shows your discomfort with your body. *Learn to shed it.* Being decent should not prevent you from being adventuresome, from being open to explore. Being genuinely decent does not stand in the way of your free and unhindered enjoyment of your lovemaking's good outcome.

First, let's be practical. As in everything we do in this life we need to make sure we are good at what we are doing, and that requires learning. We learn how to walk, how to speak, how to comport ourselves in our every day life experiences, how to study, wow to play sports. For all of these life experiences you have to learn the rules and then you need to practice before you apply your skills. It's the same for love-making which, really, is just another of our human activities, albeit by far the most intimate one. So, in order to be good at love making, learn the rules *and then put them into practice*. No one is born a good lover. You need to make yourself into one. Practice will get you there.

Beyond love-making's physical pleasures it lets you see deep into your lover's true personality, his/her likes and dislikes, his/her sensitivity, his/her fears and vulnerabilities, *and truthfulness*. There is actually a fascinating bit of wisdom in the Bible when it uses the words "to know" when in fact it says that its featured persons were simply having sex. Behind the mere semantics is the truth that nothing gives you a deeper understanding of someone's real personality than the experience of a sexual union. That has led some people to say that if you want to really get to know a person, have sex with them. This, of course, works both ways - be careful what you wish for!

The rest is just common sense:

▸ *Respect each other*. Having sex with someone for your own pleasure only is selfish and degrading. Before having sex you must be friends. Friends look out for each other and do not 'use' each other. Friends will always talk to each other.

▸ *Be intimate only when both really want to*. There has to be full and unencumbered consent on both sides. Coercion in any form has no place in personal relationships and certainly not in the most intimate of all. *Don't pressure or force anybody into sex, and let no one do it to you*. Do not seduce with false promises - be clear within yourself and with the 'Other' on the degree of commitment expected. Be sincere.

▸ *Everyone's physical needs are not the same*, and so is each person's degree of wanting to connect sex with the emotions of love. Some are comfortable with sex only in a committed relationship, needing the spiritual element of interpersonal love for their true enjoyment. Some look early in life for mates, some like to have many partners, and some take great pleasure in 'saving themselves for marriage', or waiting for their proverbial 'Knight in Shining Armor'. In any case you must respect these personal choices - they are very personal matters. Others, perhaps the more self-assured, may like something less personal, being content with 'casual' or 'recreational' sex but even then *some* level of friendship is essential for an emotionally satisfying relationship. Some are comfortable only with conventional forms, others keep looking for new experiences and new partners. Some do not need as much sex, others need a lot of it.

▸ *Don't use labels*, such as 'frigid' or 'promiscuous', there is certainly no Morality issue attached to either one state. Let's simply live according to your needs and in keeping with our upbringing. We need to be accepted for what we are. Respect everybody's preferences as long as they are the result of their free personal choices and not of coercion.

▸ *Always keep in mind* that the needs of men are not always the same as those of women. Men perhaps have a more urgent need for physical release, women a greater need for tenderness and for being wooed. Steve Harvey has put this age-old wisdom very nicely:

"*Women want to be loved, Men want to be appreciated*".

▸ *Guilt* about sexual pleasure and shame about our body's reactions are not natural states, they are imposed on us by upbringing and institutionalized beliefs. You have a right, and in fact you owe it to yourself, to follow your sexual urges as a very normal and healthy part of your private life, within the limits of the Morality of your own convictions. But yes, you should feel very guilty and ashamed if you make love selfishly, or if you talk disrespectfully about it and about your partner. Always be discreet - never talk to others about your experiences with your partners - that is just bad taste and leads to unwanted complications.

▸ *Experimenting* with new ways is fine, as long as it does not hurt or degrade or make you leave your comfort zone. Never allow yourself to be forced into anything you do not like. And there is nothing immoral about having different partners when in an uncommitted state - it is a good way to learn about other people's habits, about compatibility, physical as well as intellectual. But being insincere is immoral - do not mislead about the expected level of commitment in the relationship. Don't lie to seduce. And don't shift responsibilities for your actions:

*Your place or mine? Your place. Let **your** mother worry!*

▸ *Those who like to use drug*s including alcohol as sex enhancers or to do away with inhibitions should be reminded that they may make you do things you may later on regret. We have heard enough people say to themselves that drugs are fun only to find out later that the results become disastrous. The long term negatives far outweigh any perceived benefits. Every factual investigation into the use of drugs for seeking sexual 'highs' tells us that whatever the momentary effects may be, in the long run they are bad news.

▸ If you are seeking extra 'kicks' don't use drugs - get them from exhilaration in sports, in academics, from acting in theatre, public speaking or singing or dancing - all this can give you plenty of natural 'highs' that will pump up your adrenaline better that any drug. In any event keep your body fit with good living habits and lots of exercise. Strong and healthy bodies are indispensable prerequisites for the physical as well as the emotional success in love-making.

▸ *Find out what works for you,* and do not follow every new fad no matter how intriguing your 'Guru' may make it appear. Seek out the company of people you can like, whose values you can respect and who share your tastes. Never have sex out of desperation or to become 'popular.' Be proud of yourself and strive for the best in yourself and the people you choose to be with. When you must end a relationship do it kindly and do not play the 'blame game' - be honest from beginning to end. Honesty makes for better love-making and makes break-ups a lot less painful.

▸ *You are a unique and valuable person* deserving decency and only the best of companionship. Don't blindly imitate what others do or say. Do what is good for you and your partner. Never let other people's tastes or habits dictate your own. Have confidence in your own good judgement.

And what should our government do about these most intimate matters? Best stay out of this issue - it's too personal a matter for 'Big Government' to use its powers. It is up to our schools, our religions and social institutions and, above all, our families to set the right tone, guided by their own moral principles.

What is a Parent to do?

"Perhaps it takes courage to raise children".

(John Steinbeck, American novelist, 1902-1968)

One last signature and the beach house would be ours! Now we had our place at the sea to escape from New York's stifling summer heat.

Only a two hours drive from Manhattan our beach house was a rambling structure, built on stilts in case the sea would get too wild. It was an 'upside-down' design, the main floor with kitchen, living room and our master bedroom on the top floor. From a huge terrace you could see over the ocean forever. Below were four bedrooms with a great play room in the middle. Just right for our family, and for entertaining friends.

But first there was work to be done - scrubbing, painting, fixing the place up. And then the great opening!

Our teen-age sons had invited friends for the first weekend to help celebrate our new 'home away from home', two boys and two girls. We knew them and their parents from school meetings. One of the girls was in the youth group my wife was teaching. That girl's mother came to see us a few days before the big weekend, and after the usual niceties she came out with it: she wanted to make sure that we would take good care of her daughter and keep her safe "in every respect, you know what I mean..."

We, of course, knew quite well what she meant. We took the boys aside and laid down the law: no drinking, no smoking and no sex in our beach house. Do you understand!

Loaded down with mountains of food and drink our two-car caravan made it to our shore house in time for a great BBQ dinner. The kids built a fire on the beach in the dunes in front of the house, and from our terrace we watched them sing and dance to their guitars - a picture of a happy beach party. We let them tire themselves out until they called it a day. One more reminder: stay to yourself, and good night!

Very soon it got quiet downstairs. My wife thought it was perhaps a little too quiet. So she went down to check. In the first room, two boys fast asleep. Second room, two more, fast asleep. Third room, one girl, asleep. Fourth room, door closed, low voices - what! Knocking on the door and opening it, one boy with the girl on the bed in a warm embrace.

It turned out that both had been lovers for some time already and the girl's mother had known all along. But we understood: her mother could not possibly admit that she knew. She played by the rules - always keep up appearances.

And what did we do? We too followed the 'rules' and told the two to stay apart while they were guests in our house. Well, these two would then spend long evenings together in the dunes telling us how much they loved to admire the magnificence of the starlit nights. And what did we say to the girl's parents? Nothing. Because under the prevailing codes of behavior that was exactly what was expected.

They just preferred not to know. It was their moral code and their tacit acceptance of what was 'proper' behavior.

Like most parents you cringe at the thought that your sweet little girl and your nice young boy is becoming sexually active, that they are, well, *no longer children*. You have tried to make your young ones wait with lovemaking until they have become emotionally mature enough to fully understand their responsibilities - or at least until they would have moved out of your home. Yet no matter what you may think or try to do, you know, or should know, that they will have their youthful encounters. *'Oh no, but not **my** children'*.

Face up to it - they most likely do. It's just not good to close your eyes to this reality, but that does not prevent parents from worrying. They will always worry that their young sons and daughters may have their encounters in places that may not be
very inviting or even dangerous,  like the locker room, the backseat of a car, the abandoned shed, all places where they could run a lot of risks. So many parents find themselves in a quandary what to do when their college-age sons or daughters come home for a visit
with their 'significant other' in tow. Most parents are happy to have their visits, glad that they are comfortable enough with their parents not to hide their friends from them. But what do you say to them when they want to spend the night together in your home? And how about those young adults who are still living with their parents because this is the only way college is economically possible for them? What will you say to their lovers?

Under our prevailing moral codes, most parents will shudder at the thought of making any accommodation, afraid of the implied question on their sense of propriety and mindful of their responsibility if something would go wrong. Besides, 'what will the neighbors say'? In her book "Not under my Roof", Amy Schalet, a world-renowned social researcher, makes the point that it all depends how much trust the parents have in the level of maturity of their young ones. But our present concept of what is proper behavior is still heavily influenced by the remnants from our Puritan heritage that makes most of us terribly uncomfortable with the idea of allowing sexual encounters 'under our roof' .

What then to do about our young people's new habit of exchanging sexual messages via internet and cellphone, the much discussed 'sexting' and 'cyber-erotics'? As you would expect from our young tech-savvy youngsters they will use all the new media at hand, just as we older ones used whatever communication technology was available in our days. As with all previous generations it is futile to stem that tide by edict, by censure, or by outright prohibition. None of that has ever worked, even when enforced by hugely disproportionate penalties. Much better to teach them to use the 'Delete' button on undesirable and unwanted messages.

And what about the deplorable 'cyber-bullying'? These are not just youthful pranks. 'Bullying' in any form, in any place is should be unacceptable in our communities, any where. It needs drastic corrective action on grounds that it interferes with the victims' human rights. There are voices from legal circles that suggest criminal prosecution especially when such cyber-bullying has shamed victims into suicide - this is one one good case where government intervention is indeed justified.

Then there is the awkward matter of pornography. Everybody proclaims disdain, but the plain fact is that pornography continues to be commercially successful no matter what is done to suppress it. Clearly, pornography is not a good way for young people to learn about sex - it is denigrating a wonderful part of our lives. As much as many of us would like to see it kept out of the hands of young people, our modern countries' concept of freedom of expression makes all forms of censorship moot.

Let's not get too worked up over pornography - it may be distasteful for you, but (other than for immature youngsters) does it really do that much harm? At least some people get enjoyment from it, whether we like this stuff or not. Some criminologists do see a link between excessive use of pornography and sex crimes, but they also have shown clear evidence that exposure to violence and brutality in our movies and video games entice violent crime. That is where our moral indignation - and our laws - should be at least equally directed.

There is no easy answer. Parents must not be afraid to use the parental controls features on the common electronics, but too often our youngster know quite well how to bypass them. The more important measure is to make our young ones understand that no matter how they communicate with each other, they should do so with a clear understanding of their moral obligations to uphold human decency and respect for the other's privacy. Sex, like all other human relations, must never be made into something uncomfortable or insulting. There never is a place for anything disparaging or denigrating - that is where the lines must be drawn. Teach them that protecting the feelings of the other must be above their own desires, simply as a matter of common decency.

There are indeed limits to our cherished personal freedoms when we abuse them by insulting others to a point where it can potentially destroy their reputations or even their lives. Our personal sense of Morality should prevent us from such trespasses. This is an area that would justify appropriate public policy making, a good field for government to step in to protect the vulnerable from harm.

The Disaster when Sex and Politics mix

A party! We were were invited to a birthday party! The neighbors' daughter was turning eighteen. It was the summer of 1942. The war had been dragging on and had come to our town with long nights in the bomb shelter and the endless lines for our meager rations. It was beginning to wear us down.

Now a party! Perhaps there would be a small cake, a little juice and for the grown-ups perhaps a cup of 'Ersatz' coffee. We knew we could not expect more. That did not matter. I rehearsed the little poem I was to recite as my birthday present.

In spite of all the turmoil of the war around us, her parents had kept life inside her family as normal as possible. I still remember how they had decorated their home. Flowers everywhere, the table set with their fine china, embroidered table cloth and matching napkins - a 'gemuetlich' German middle class setting.

We sang, we recited, we drank and we ate the delicious cake. Her father broke out the brandy he had saved for this occasion for the grown-ups. Happiness all around.

The birthday girl stood up. Glowing with pride she announced "I have signed up with the Lebensborn to have a baby for our Fuehrer and our Vaterland!"

For a moment there was stunned silence. It was as though we were frozen on our chairs. Her father glared at her trying to understand. "What did you say?" was all he could get out. Again: "What did you say?"

Not quite so sure of herself any more she said "well, now that I am eighteen I am able to do my duty to my country".

Her parents looked at each other in disbelief. Then all hell broke loose, her mother crying hysterically and her father, red in the face, thundering "how could you do such a thing, are you out of your mind?"

They could not believe it. Here stood their daughter, in their eyes still their sweet little girl, in her youthful determination to do what her Group Leader had put into her head - to have a baby for her country.

They would not have any of this. No way. "You go right now and tell your Leader that you are not going to do this, no way!"

Defiant, looking her father straight into the eye she yelled: "Nobody, not you, not anybody, will keep me from doing my duty! And I will tell my Leader what you said!"

At that, everybody fell silent. Would she really go as far as to denounce her parents? So may others had done this awful thing. We knew what that meant - interrogations, stern warnings at best, and very possibly a lot worse. Marked an 'Enemy of the Vaterland' her father would be removed from his position, and then what?

The party was over. Everybody left in shocked silence. Her father shook hands with his friends who looked deeply into his eyes signaling their full support. Her mother giving her sobbing friends a warm embrace. That was all that could be done. But it meant much for all of us.

Unlike so many other very sad stories from Nazi Germany this one had a happy ending - sort of. This girl finally saw the light and did rescind her commitment. She did not denounce her parents. Her solid upbringing in a family with sound morals had made the difference. Perhaps seeing that other parents fully supported hers in this matter may have helped also, underlining the positive reinforcement that can come from a community who had kept its basic decency and conservative morals.

In their unfathomable Immorality, the Nazis had created the 'Lebensborn' in the middle of WWII in response to Germany's staggering human losses. It was an institution where soldiers meeting the Nazi criteria of the 'Master Race' would be invited to impregnate young girls. Their babies would be given up to   special orphanages to be raised to become good Nazis - and cannon fodder for future wars - a flagrant case of the State imposing its morbid concept of Morality on brain-washed young people who simply no longer knew better.

A clear-cut case of personal morals in conflict with the state's that naturally can only happen in a dictatorship, right? But not so fast: even here and now there is an ongoing dispute in some quarters whether the state should have a role in determining what is moral and what is not. Some ultra-conservative groups, often guided by faith-based concepts, make the case that "the obligations of Government are to protect public health, safety *and morals*" [emphasis added] as stated, for example, by Robert P. George, law professor at

Princeton University, one of the leading spokesmen for the conservative camp. It is difficult to argue these premises until we come to the question what exactly is meant by "protecting morals" - does that really mean that moral standards are indeed to be set and then presumably *policed* by 'Government'? Would that not inevitably lead to censorship to 'protect' the public from exposure to what 'Government' declares to be immoral? And would this not give 'Government' powers totally beyond what is laid down in our Constitution?

In a modern society it is pretty much agreed that Morality as such should not be legislated. Yet, it is true also that exclusive reliance on our inner conscience alone is not always a sufficient safeguard to protect the weak and the powerless from exploitation. This is especially important for saving children from abuse by those in charge of their education and training. For their protection there is an undisputed need for legislation, but there are fundamental ideologic differences between the progressive and the conservative camps on how to do this. In progressive societies Morality-related legislation makes violence, coercion, abuse and harassment illegal not only on grounds of immorality *but as a matter of human rights*. In the conservative camp, legislation continues to be pursued on the basis of faith-based dogmas on how they think people should live their lives.

In considering legislation on sexual matters, the conservative camp focusses on the 'natural' concept saying that since the ultimate purpose of sex is reproduction, anything that does not fit into the 'way it's supposed to be' should be considered 'un-natural' *and therefor immoral*. Following this path to its ultimate logical conclusion inevitably leads to outlawing contraceptives, abortion and homosexuality on grounds that all these activities are thwarting reproduction in one way or another. By contrast, the progressive camp looks at sex as a pleasurable body function that has intrinsic moral value. For them what divides the permissible from the objectionable is the question whether *real* (as opposed to imagined) *harm* is done to the participants or to the community.

Laws dealing with matters of personal behavior are justified when their purpose is to protect the weak from harm. By contrast, laws that impose faith-based dogmas that are subscribed to by some of us on the rest of the population always lead to oppression and hypocrisy. In our present time we are in the midst of a single minded legislative drive by the conservative camp to establish government controls on such personal choices as contraceptives, abortion or same-sex unions.

There is probably no other area of our very personal lives that is as hotly contested as the issue of abortion. Of course, nobody is comfortable with taking a fetus' life. The highly charged debate is about who should have the power to decide on an abortion - government with its laws, as vehemently insisted upon by the 'conservative', mainly 'faith based' camp, or the woman carrying the child (and her doctor), as equally vehemently defended by the 'progressive' camp. This is not easy. The more sensible way to deal with this thorny issue is to find ways to prevent unwanted pregnancies to begin with, like counseling on reproduction, by appropriate sex education and by making contraceptives more easily available.

Trying to solve this problem with ideologically driven legislation would be tantamount to 'regulate' the private lives of people. It would allow 'government' to reach into our most personal matters, and thus would make government even 'bigger' in areas where government certainly should not be. Ironically, the same political groups that are adamantly promoting such government invasion into our private lives are the very same who are riling against 'Big Government' when it puts in place regulations to protect the public from the harm that comes from pollution, from our environment being ravaged, and from destructive financial manipulations. Is that saying that 'Big Government' is *good* when it tries to control our very personal lives, but 'Big Government' is *bad* when it tries to protect its people from harm?

It will be difficult to overcome these contradictions as long as our political discourse is dominated by ideology rather than by rational examination. Our Constitution protects the right of all of us to live our private lives according to our own choices, rather than by government edicts driven by some vocal ideologists.

It is just another reason why in our modern world politics and sex should not be allowed to mix.

What Is 'Proper' Moral Behavior ?

"When in Rome do as the Romans"
(Attributed to Saint Augustine when a visitor from abroad asked for advice how to cope with the habits of the Romans)

A few years ago my wife was standing at a corner of Rome's Via Veneto waiting to cross the street when a newly arrived American girl standing next to her got pinched on her bottom. Incensed, the young woman hit the handsome young Italian with her purse, leaving his face - and his feelings - slightly bruised. The Carabinieri arrived and after a lively verbal exchange arrested the girl. To give her some support my wife volunteered to accompany her to the police station. The judge asked why she had hit the young man - "well, he had pinched me!". The judge shook his head: "Yes, I heard that, but again, why did you hit him?"

Other countries, other habits: 'Groping' is not allowed in almost all societies but in some otherwise civilized countries pinching women, while mostly not welcomed, is not a criminal offense - some men consider it a compliment to a woman's beauty! In Italy, when a stranger is enchanted by your beautiful eyes and says "bel ochio" it would never be considered offensive but would most probably be classified as harassment here.

Every culture has its own set of rules of 'proper' behavior. Within each culture what is acceptable behavior will vary very much depending on the particular circumstances - whether it is in public, among friends, or in the work place. No matter how explicitly stated, the 'official' versions of these rules are not always easy to deal with - stumbling over these rules may become comical - or a real offense. Your safest guide in navigating this maze is a basic respect for the prevailing rules and sensitivity for the feelings of others.

What is considered 'sexual harassment' is ultimately a matter of very personal reactions to suggestive remarks, off-color jokes, or 'inappropriate' touching. In one set of circumstance, such as at a lively party, that could be laughed off but in another setting such as the work place it can indeed be offensive. But what about flirting or good old-fashioned *wooing*? When does that become harassment? Is it harassment when a man persists in asking a woman to marry him hoping one day she may say the hoped-for '*YES*'?

Clearly, unwanted sexual advances are immoral, but so are the abuses of these laws by frivolous accusations of harassment, by inventing or exaggerating events that do not rise to the level of the protection intended by the law - this is equally immoral. So is our paranoid persecution of public figures for their alleged or real personal trespasses - we elect them for their expertise and their willingness to serve the community and in that capacity they should be judged solely on their performance in their job, not on their degree of chastity. Like everyone else they are accountable for their personal choices only to themselves and their families. Moreover, a commitment to sexual purity is not a part of the job description for our officials, but honesty and immunity to bribery certainly is.

Here is a huge disconnect in our moral judgements. With our ill-placed moralizing we often resort to questionable ways to ferret out such trespasses, or to even provoke them - what is a 'sting operation' to one is 'entrapment' to another, with a very fine moral line separating the two. Where is our sense of fairness? Do we need government to step in with ever more complicated rules and laws, or is it a matter of improving our personal sense of common decency? Maybe those who are doing too much moralizing may actually thereby reveal inner conflicts about their own hidden inclinations.

Certainly it is totally *immoral* to pounce on others with the intent to get them into trouble over their very personal habits, even when practiced in private *with consenting adults*. To willfully destroy someone's reputation, family and career on these grounds is despicable, especially when the shaming of hapless victims leads to suicide. Where in all of this is our time-honored concept of "presumed innocent until proven guilty"? Have we come to a point where we routinely assume that just the *accusation* of misconduct is enough to establish guilt, shifting the burden of proof to the accused?

But how about state secrets being put at risk as a result of sexual misconduct among people of importance, and are they not opening themselves to all kinds of blackmail with their illicit behavior? But it is precisely our own moralizing about such missteps that the opportunity for damaging blackmail is created. Indeed, 'state secrets' are leaked all the time without any need for setting traps with sex. Money usually does a fine job in buying secrets, and it is a remarkably inefficient way to pry out secrets from a lover - it is the stuff of spy movies more than of real life. And have we totally forgotten that in most jurisdictions, blackmail and extortion are considered criminal offenses? Why do we tend to condemn the *victims* of blackmail and extortion, instead of the blackmailers ?

The New Morality wants us to look beyond the issues of personal conduct and to place at least as much scrutiny on proper behavior of our government agencies. Why waste so much time and effort on salacious sex scandals when the much bigger problems in our communities come from morally questionable public policy decision making?

Morals, the Arts and Censorship

With a heavy heart he took one more look at his gallery. For three generations his family had been leading members of the Viennese art community, respected for their integrity in dealing with Vienna's much treasured painters. In the best tradition of their gallery his family had used its wealth to support many struggling young artist like Egon Schiele, Kokoschka and Gustav Klimt, paving their way into the mainstream art world.

But now trouble had come to his beloved Vienna. Nazi Germany had annexed Austria and with it came the Nazis' insane persecution of the Jews - and that meant the end of his famed art gallery. It did not matter to the Nazi thugs that he was the scion of an old established family that had been a major part of Vienna's cultural life for generations. They were prominent civic leaders, supporting the arts and many Viennese charities. They loved their Austria. They were patriots, their men had served with distinction in the Great War's Imperial Army. Now they would be declared outlaws, soon to become fugitives from their own country.

With a sigh of resignation he took down the smaller of his paintings, those that he could carry with him on his long journey that eventually would be taking him and his young family to the safety of America. The Nazis would confiscate his remaining possessions.

New art has aways been controversial - it would not be *new* if it would not be so. From the days of el Greco to Goya and to the French impressionists, all were first viewed with disdain by the art establishment of their times until they became revered parts of our cultural lives. Art in its many forms would go in and out of fashion, even religious art. With every new art came disputes about its spiritual values and its Morality, especially when depicting the human body in provocative poses.

Censorship was the Nazis' way to 'protect' their citizens from the moral harm they imagined would come to them from modern art. Like all dictators they wanted to control what others think and do. Not content with just outlawing whatever displeased them they would burn books and confiscate art, mostly not even understanding it. Those who would resist would be thrown into their concentration camps. As it was discovered later, many of the Nazi thugs were drooling behind closed doors over some of the more erotic pieces of art they had stolen, and the more enjoyment they got from them, the more vicious they became in prosecuting the artists.

The Nazis were the ultimate hypocrites - the inevitable outcome when politics tries to determine what is moral and what is not. When it came to art they liked the pretext of safeguarding the national moral 'innocence' from the 'Degenerates'. But most important: it showed their total disconnect from all matters of Morality. They would get all worked up over the 'Immorality' of some explicit images of the human body, and at the same time they were unable - or unwilling - to see the enormous *Immorality* of their barbaric treatment of the Jewish people. *The mindset of the Nazis was their all-encompassing Immorality.*

Now 'fast-forward' five decades in time. The Viennese art dealer's son had discovered that Klimt's world-famous "Fulfillment" (the third part of Klimt's tryptic with "The Kiss" and "The Expectation") had found its way to the Strasbourg Art Museum. He remembered well that it had hung in his parents' Vienna living room. Like many other dispossessed former owners of significant art, he wanted it back - not for its enormous value - his family did not need the money, but as a matter of principle. Like with so many other restitution efforts he encountered the typical artificial roadblocks which raised many questions about legality and fairness, about the Morality of it all - and about politics :

▸ The Strasbourg Art Museum did not want to part with its prized possession. Their Klimt hung prominently in the Museum's main hall. As expected, the Museum claimed it had been acquired legally.

▸ The citizens of Strasbourg were proud to have it in their city. The mayor knew that letting it go back to its original owner would anger many of his constituents. Afraid he might lose his re-election over this issue, he publicly defended his Museum's position.

▸ Keenly aware of the political currents among his fellow citizens, the local municipal judge demanded tangible 'proof of ownership'. Of course, everybody knew that this would be impossible to get - to cover their tracks the Nazis had routinely destroyed all ownership records. Yes, there were markings on the painting's frame and on its shipping crate that could be traced back to the former gallery, but the judge declared them to be 'insufficient circumstantial evidence'.

We went to the Regional French Court of Appeals. Unencumbered by local politics it looked beyond the phony technicalities of 'Proof of Ownership' by examining the painting's history in its entirety. Witnesses confirmed that the paining indeed had hung in his father's home, and that because of the paintings enormous size, he could not possibly have carried it away, given that he was under such close Nazi surveillance at that time. The Appeals Court also noted that the price at which the Museum had acquired the Klimt in 1959 was "derisively" low - $7,000 - which should have made the Museum doubt the legitimacy of the seller.

The court's decision to widen its deliberations beyond the technicality of the proof-of-ownership issue put the *moral judgement* into the center of the discussions. The Court finally ordered the painting to be turned over to the art dealer's heirs. Once again in possession of this great piece of art, they decided to donate it to a charitable organization supporting promising young artists. This is what they believed their father would have done for his Viennese arts community. *It was a morally admirable outcome of all the painting's meandering and a fitting rebuke of the Nazi culture of Immorality.*

Beware of all forms of censorship. The more ardent the censorship the more we should question the censors' real motives. More often than not you will find that their moralizing is far from sincere.

There are many Sides to Sex

"That is not a just government where arbitrary restrictions deny a part of its Citizens that free use of their faculties ....."

(James Madison, 4th President of the USA from 1809 to 1817)

Where are the limits to the right of peoples' personal choices of the "use of their faculties"?

You can ask this question about the sad fact of prostitution, male and female, considered by many as an insult to the human spirit and to boot a primary source of STD, and unpardonable when it involves children. Not only the Bible but countless stories tell us that prostitution existed throughout history, judged by most of us as a threat to human dignity and especially to the stability of the family.

Why is prostitution still around everywhere in the world? The simple fact is that when sex is not available men will seek release somewhere, and lonely women will have their 'escorts' to give them the attention they seek. It is not just a matter of a lack of good morals but the result of unfulfilled human needs. Simply declaring prostitution illegal has never succeeded in making it disappear. It just is driving it underground, making it a haven for pimps and other criminals. Some countries tried to solve the legal issues by making it a criminal offense for a man to pay for sex but not for the woman offering her services. No matter how it is dealt with, wherever prostitution is made illegal it leads to abominable forms of human trafficking and slavery, and has been so throughout the ages.

Recently quite a few countries have come to the conclusion, albeit reluctantly, that prostitution is a reality that needs to be acknowledged. Instead of simply moralizing about it they try to establish a legal and social framework to make it somewhat manageable. Their main objective is to keep criminals out and to provide regular medical examinations to control the spread of STD. There is even a new term for it: "Sex Workers", who actually are included in some countries' social security and health insurance schemes.

Our own society's attitudes on prostitution are often two-faced - many of us are vociferous in its condemnation and yet we love to see old-fashioned brothels in a romantic light, as in our Western frontier movies and in innumerable books, giving these institutions more credit than they deserve. One can understand the frustration of our law enforcement officers with our ambivalence and the glaring contradictions in our prostitution laws. This was expressed quite bluntly by a New York police inspector in the days of Teddy Roosevelt's ill-fated campaign to fight crime in the city. When attacked for condoning (and profiting from) brothels, he declared that "they serve a good purpose because they keep prostitutes off the streets".

How big is this problem today in our society? A periodic University of Chicago survey funded by the National Science Foundation shows that in 2012 about 9 percent of all participating males stated that they had paid for sex - that compares with over 17 percent just 20 years ago. These researchers found that this favorable trend is mainly due to the fact that 'legitimate' sex has generally become more easily available. Those who equate its easier availability with 'loose morals' should at least consider the benefit of reducing the dependency on prostitution for so many.

Social psychologists suggest that we should be realistic in this matter and that we should look at prostitution not so much as a moral but as a social hygiene issue. In any event it doesn't help if we close our eyes to the existence of 'sex workers' - they are indeed all around us. In addition, some legitimate treatments like various types of 'sex therapy' have already started to blur the lines of moral considerations in this area. For example, it is difficult to see anything immoral in therapy aimed at curing sexual dysfunctions. In the end, what is acceptable and what is not depends on the intended outcome, whether something good is being achieved or whether real harm is done.

Many local politicians love to play 'tough on crime' in their rhetoric on prostitution. For them it is a safe way of garnering votes - no one wants to challenge them on this issue. But very few politicians have the guts to call it what it really is - a public health issue that should be treated as such, and not as a 'crime'.

"Falling madly in Love" - enjoy, but beware!

"Oh, that it would forever keep blossoming,
this magical time of young love!"
   (Friedrich Schiller 1788-1805, German poet of Freedom)

Everybody loves the story of Romeo and Juliette, the epitome of a sweet romance and youthful passion but, of course, no one likes the tragic outcome of their legendary love affair. But it still happens all the time - two youngsters falling in love, head-over-heels, often forgetting the world around them, their families, the rules of behavior of their times, even sometimes resorting to drugs, and too often ending in tragedy for both. We are in awe of their all-consuming passion, and we shed tears for them when they despair over their disappointments, when they think their lives are falling apart. But what are the real life lessons?

Those of us who had the good fortune of the exhilarating experience of falling deeply in love at a young age will remember the giddiness of being on top of the world. Who would not want to have this overpowering feeling of sweetness and the waves of emotions of an all-consuming love? Being 'in love' is one of life's most wonderful sensations. When it happens you should just enjoy and make it the best time of your life.

We know, of course, that there is a big difference between 'Falling in Love' versus true loving. Falling in love, the magical lightning-like infatuation, will suddenly draw a couple together in great passion so strong that they simply cannot be without each other. 'Love sickness' setting in especially when not consummated. Emotions and desire run so high that all restraints and social conventions are forgotten, the lovers blinded to any imperfections or problems. Lacking experience, love-making is usually frenzied with all precautions thrown to the wind. Anthropologists say that this type of out-of-control love-making is nature's way to ensure reproduction of the species. It simply is creating a state of mind where all hesitations about the physiological and social consequences are temporarily discarded.

Can real love even exist at a very young age? Indeed it can. It can be so much more powerful than the love experienced by older persons because it is not yet tempered by the realities of life. Unfortunately, so many young people make terrible mistakes in this state, especially when they assume that their infatuation will mature into an enduring relationship. When it does it can lead to a long life together in bliss. But the world is full of Romeo and Juliette-type tragedies. We may be in rapture at the image of overpowering passionate love but the outcome of 'blind love' can be different from its great expectations. Too many young people rush into unsuitable long term commitments, especially when society makes it too difficult to consummate their youthful passions other than by getting married - which is surely getting married for the wrong reasons. Sensible sex education could be helpful to prevent such unfortunate happenings. The politics of suppressing efforts to properly inform our young ones on the realities of our lives are not doing us - and them - any favors.

> *"When falling in love, you don't see faults in your lover,*
> *Real love is when your lover's faults don't too much bother".*

(Johann Wolfgang Goethe, 1749-1832, playwright, statesman, scientist).

Jealousy, Maddening Jealousy!

"The Jealous are troublesome to others
but a torment to themselves"
(William Penn, Early American colonist, 1644-1718)

In his tragedy about Othello, Shakespeare tells the story how Othello's 'friend' Iago sets out to sow doubts in Othello's mind about his beloved  Desdemona's faithfulness, the only evidence being her handkerchief having found its way into the wrong hands. It took less than forty lines of Shakespeare's writing skills to make Othello mad enough with jealousy to set into motion one of the world's great literary tragedies.

Jealousy strikes in many life relationships, whenever you feel that another person is unjustly favored over you. You think your teacher likes the student next to you more than you, gives her better grades. At work your boss praises a co-worker for work you think you did better. And then, of course, you see the person you love flirting with someone else. You quickly see the possibility of infidelity, and you may in fact discover some form of betrayal. That hurts terribly. You become unhappy with yourself, furious with everybody that you think has done you wrong, no longer interested or capable of seeing things in a reasonable perspective. Jealousy makes life miserable for you and everybody around you.

In terms of psychology, jealousy is closely related to envy, one of the self-destructive 'Seven Deadly Sins'. But unlike envy, jealousy is the result of a hurt inflicted upon you by someone out there, whether real or imagined. The 'real' part giving cause for jealousy has something tangible to deal with, and you can take sensible action, as painful as it may be. The 'imagined' part is quite something else. It is hard to say when you are justified or not, but always think of Shakespeare's Iago and how easy it was for Othello to fall prey to imagined or suggested offenses. Just be careful not to jump to conclusions. It may hurt you more than the real thing.

Jealousy is sometimes different for men and women. Men's jealousies are often driven by their 'alpha-male' syndrome, incensed by the loss of a companion to somebody else, some men still looking at their mates as something of a possession. For women, the fear of abandonment, of being left alone to fend for themselves (and their children) is understandably one of their deeper causes of jealousy.

Innumerable crimes of violence are committed in the wake of jealousy's emotional nightmares, starting with wife-beating and ending too often in murder. In some jurisdictions much leeway is given in cases of 'crimes of passion'. But allowing mitigating circumstances for crimes of passion leads to a slippery slope of highly subjective legal maneuvers, very much like the much abused excusatory claims of insanity in criminal cases - of course you can always say that in committing a capital offense "you must have been out of your mind" but this should not be construed as an excuse.

Deep-seated jealousy is usually more about our own insecurities than about those we profess to love. It is born from our natural interest in self-preservation, and sometimes plain selfishness - that is a Cardinal Sin. And the worst kind of jealousy is that which is created artificially, just for the purpose of hurting the other. *That is highly immoral.*

On Nakedness And Nudity

A little boy visiting the YWCA with his mother, gets lost and inadvertently opens the door to the women's locker room. The women scream, running for towels to cover themselves. The little boy, perplexed, asks "Haven't you ever seen a little boy before?"

It seems natural that we are a bit squeamish about our naked bodies, but why has it become such an obsession that it has led to censorship and quirky attitudes, equating shows of nakedness with wickedness, with an unsavory intent to arouse? Most societies have established the concept of 'modesty' as a virtue, thinking that images of our naked bodies might damage our emotional and physical health. This concept of 'modesty' has made us strangely sensitive about our naked bodies beyond all reason. But even the Vatican - of all places - is full of nakedness in its much treasured art.

In the heyday of British colonialism the High Commissioner's wife was accompanying her husband on a visit to a native festival. Appalled when the girls' dancing group lifted up their grass skirts, thereby exposing their naked private parts, she angrily turned on her husband - defending himself he assured her that the girls had been carefully instructed to always cover their breasts.....

Even in our modern environment, we still act prudish when it comes to the realities of our bodies, perhaps because we keep confusing the sights of nakedness with promiscuity and with the intent to arouse. Sometimes that may be true, but it is always the intent that counts, not the amount of human skin offered to our eyes. Maybe gradually we will learn to make this distinction and become more tolerant and less offended by shows of the body, and overcome our discomfort with it, whether real or pretended.

The latest uproar here about the new 'show it all' airport screening devices is indicative that so many of us still have a paranoid fear of 'being seen', a relic of mores that to most moderns are archaic and totally missing the point. *Decency has nothing to do with how much or how little clothing you wear.* Lack of decency is when you do things that are willfully shocking, insulting or embarrassing to others. In case of doubt, wear as much or as little clothing just as the rest of the people around you do. In matters of nudity it makes no sense to provoke. This is an example where it is best to be conformist. If you do not like what people around you wear or do, just go some place else where people's habits are more to your liking.

One recent example of this disconnect of moral judgements about nudity came to us as a result of the now infamous case of the 'Wardrobe Malfunction' at the occasion of a televised sports event when a less-than-a-second accidental showing of a woman's breast led to several years of court actions, *right up to the US Supreme Court.* This out-of proportion reaction was caused by some people who thought that this had put their children in great moral danger. The same people totally ignored that at the same time millions of children were exposed to thousands of shows of gross violence and brutality on TV or in video games. Psychologists agree that exposure to graphic violence does infinitely greater harm to children than nine-sixteenth of a second of a tiny image of a human breast. Perhaps, the discomfort with our bodies is a left-over from our Puritan heritage being still very much alive in so many of us.

The story is told of a New York City dowager who filed a complaint against a couple living across the Avenue for not drawing their curtains while making love. In her testimony she said that in spite of her bad eyesight she could see it quite clearly when she used her binoculars.....

The 'Nudity Movement' is a somewhat different story. To be casual about being nude is one thing, to make nudity a social program is another. People join nudist groups for many different reasons. Some may truly enjoy the freedom from clothing, some may be voyeurs, some seek sexual excitement, and most of them probably some mix of all that. Interestingly many nudists become quite defensive when asked why they do it, praising the purity of their hobby with somewhat suspect ardor, a little like "Thou protests too much...." Whatever their real motives, let them do what seems to make them happy, as long as nobody is forced into it.

Of course, there are shows of nudity that are meant to shock or insult or threaten, and those should be abhorred. But let's not be so 'up-tight' about it by making it into a bigger deal than it really is. Even when a perverse male 'exposes' himself it can be more effective to laugh at it than to go to court where an innocent victim may have to testify. Especially for children, this may turn out to be a lot more harmful than the unfortunate experience of the exposure itself. Sometimes it is better to treat this type of transgression as a sick joke rather than as a criminal offense.

As always in matters of moral judgements, the deciding question is whether real harm has been done. It is sometimes a bit suspicious when shows of nudity are made into a big Morality issue - this may draw more attention to it than necessary. Also, please be reminded that you don't have to look. And if it comes to you electronically you can make good use of the great convenience of the 'Delete' button.

There is indeed a need for legislation to protect our children from harm. However, any attempts to solve this issue also requires fostering a better sense of common decency, by our schools, our institutions and above all, by our families.

Are You Ready For A Lasting Relationship?

"Marriage is the will of Two to create a One
which is more than the Two who created it".
(Friedrich Nietzsche, German philosopher, 1844-1900)

You have found your love. You have become best friends. You want to be together all the time, to build a life together, nurture each other's interests and needs. Your love-making is deeply satisfying. You know how to laugh together. You are a team, supporting each other in your endeavors and careers, generously making sure that whatever you do must further your common good, your mutual spiritual and physical well-being. You are sharing chores fairly, each pulling his or her weight in keeping life vibrant. You have seen that neither of you is perfect but you have learned how to overcome your differences. You want to support each other and to be there for each other at all times, no matter what the situation may be, even when there are occasional problems between the two of you.

Then you will want to make a commitment of permanent exclusivity, fully aware that with that decision many of life's rules change, definitely. You should make that commitment only when you are prepared to honor its promise, *no if's or but's*, whether your commitment is in the form of the traditional marriage, or a personal pledge, a 'civil union', or as recently introduced in some countries, a 'term' marriage:

If you commit yourself you should be faithful to each other.

Being unfaithful in a committed state is a breach of trust and an affront to the spirit. It disrupts the security of being able to rely on each other in life's ups and downs and it especially affects children. Even common decency should prevent you from causing grief to your partner in life. It should also be a matter of personal honor, as old-fashioned as it may sound. Remember that with commitment comes the promise of exclusivity. It is the bedrock of a successful and enduring relationship. Even in our modern world there is no better alternative.

Those who think there are other ways to live as a couple are simply chasing a rainbow. For one, the idea of 'open marriage' is a pipe dream. It simply does not work - we humans are not built that way, neither emotionally nor physically. Aside from being illegal in the civilized world, polygamy is, of course, fundamentally unacceptable; it is an insult to the partners' integrity and also because it is based on the concept of inequality of the sexes. Nobody should waste their time - and potentially risk a good relationship - by even thinking about such outlandish aberrations or 'experimenting' with them. Some of these life styles make for tantalizing books or movies but they are not anywhere near reality. Pursuing these sometimes tempting venues are not worth the risk of the inevitable unintended consequences.

It's a simple truth: when you are in a committed state, sexual exclusivity is an essential ingredient for the success of the relationship. However, we should never lose sight that a marriage must be much more than about sex, as important and elevating as it may be. Sex alone should not define a marriage because much beyond is the ideal of wanting to go through this life together. To get married just to have sex is a terrible idea; it actually denigrates the much more lofty concept of a union of two persons.

A marriage must be based on a spiritual union, on the will to build a family, to live decently together in the community. The key condition for a marriage to work is that both partners must be there for each other at all times to nurture each other's physical and emotional needs. Sexual exclusivity is a hugely important part of this, but there are so many other ways to be 'unfaithful'. It is amazing how confused people can be about this:

Responding to the social worker's question why he thought his wife had left him he said he did not know: "OK, so I have beaten her a few times but so what! I have always been faithful to her."

But then you will ask what to do when in spite of the best intentions a committed partner is unfaithful. For most of us this is a serious violation of trust and commitment with painful disappointment and anger to follow. However, let not your emotions make you rash decisions that you may regret. Don't just let it happen that you will 'fall out of love' - too often it is just the result of not making enough of an effort to make the union a success. Don't only follow your emotions - use your head also.

The renowned marriage counselor Dr. Barry Ginsberg gave a lot of thought how people cope - or fail to cope - with the problem of infidelity. He finds that there is a big difference between giving in to the temptation of a 'one-night stand', and the much more damaging longer-term 'affair'. He considers 'affairs' a much more serious matter because they involve a higher level of commitment to another person, thus shifting loyalty away from your marriage partner. 'One-night stands' do not necessarily carry with them this threat. 'Affairs' come an awful lot closer to real betrayal and therefore threaten the personal intimacy of a couple on a deeper level, *even when sex is not involved.*

He also concurs that 'extra-marital' affairs have different aspects for women as for men. In her in-depth examination of attitudes about infidelity, the eminent Dr. Meredith Chivers, Professor of Psychology at Queens College had this to say (in paraphrase):

Nothing describes better the difference between men and women in their respective attitudes on infidelity than the man's typical defense "it meant nothing to me" and the woman's retort "if it meant nothing to you then why did you do it?" It leaves you to ponder what is more likely to rock a marriage's foundation - a 'meaningless' one-night stand or a 'meaningful' affair. It is the 'meaningful' in an affair that strikes at the core of a marriage, at the union of soul mates. It would demonstrate to your mate that you prefer to be with another person.

In Ginsberg's essay on "Improving Couples' Attachment Security and Satisfaction" he concludes that the chances to overcome the damage done to a marriage by infidelities depends on the overall quality of the couples' relationship. In essence he says that if the partners genuinely liked each other and have conducted themselves decently in their everyday life together, then both can have a good chance to come to terms with infidelity. Help can also come from supportive friends and from religions - if they truly put into practice what they preach about compassion and forgiveness.

How can there ever again be a trusting relationship again, the 'attachment security' that Dr. Ginsberg is talking about? It boils down to a simple question: What is more important for you - breaking up because of a less than perfect fidelity record or resuming your life together as you wanted to begin with?

Never throw away a marriage thoughtlessly and without examination of the alternatives. "A marriage has a great value in itself, and we should never cause it to be lost when it can be saved with a manageable effort on both sides", as the famed feminist, Elaine Sciolino, former New York Times Paris Bureau Chief, once put it: "You have established your foundation as a couple, you have a history together, *a marriage*. You have built something of great value to be proud of and you should not allow imperfections or regrettable transgressions disrupt it".

Let's face it: when people run for the divorce court over sexual missteps they are often using them as a subterfuge because they want to get out of a relationship for some entirely different reason, like dissatisfaction with the everyday living together, or ambitions to do something else with their lives. There are good reasons that our legal process is usually not making it easy to get a divorce - creating in effect a waiting period simply as a result of 'red tape'. A formal request for a 'waiting period' can be a very good move.

But what then are the real causes for a marriage to fail? It usually is the final result of an accumulation of everyday violations of basic rules of decency in the conduct between the partners. So often sexual infidelity is just the 'tipping point' that pushes an already damaged relationship over the top. Infidelity is routinely used as a front to hide the real causes of a couple having grown apart. But there are so many other ways to be in effect 'unfaithful' - by too many unkind words, snide remarks, fights about money or status, recurring angry arguments, public humiliation and criticism of your partner, or by simply choosing to spend your time with friends rather than with your spouse.

What makes marriage succeed? Work together to make life pleasant for each other:

To have a good spouse, be a good spouse.

Laugh a lot *with* each other, but never *at* the other. Keep the home front at peace - for most of us it is impossible to have romance in our married life when there is too much tension, most of which can be avoided by simply being kind to each other. It pays huge dividends.

Of course, it is always easy to be nice when things go well, but the true strength of our character shows when life gets stressful and when we find it difficult to be kind to each other. Make a conscious effort not to give in to the temptation of speaking harsh or insulting words especially when you are angry. *Anger is a bad counsellor.*

Innumerable books are sold on 'relationships', how to create them, how to improve and maintain them. Some of them give good practical advice, but some are trying to be overly sophisticated. Some are making use of a very large body of teachings on human psychology, psychiatry and religion, and some take a more medical approach. But things do not have to be so complicated. In most real-life, every-day situations, just remember some very simple and time-honored rules that help avoid unnecessary damages to your relationship, such as:

- *Before you say something hurtful, just count to ten.*

- *Just stop talking when an argument is about to escalate.*

Above all, just accept that none of us are perfect, not only in matters of sexual exclusivity, but also in the way we give of ourselves in our every day actions. When trouble comes ask yourself whether you really have been as supportive as you should be, whether you have been a real team player or whether perhaps you fell for the temptation too often to criticize or be sarcastic:

> *Sarcasm is the poison pill for any relationship.*
>
> *And so is nagging,*
>
> *And so is bringing up old hurts over and over again.*

As so often, the simplest guidelines are the best:

> *Be at least as nice and as polite to your spouse as you*
> *would be to any stranger,*
> *and always be ready to forgive.*

Marriage is the state in which love in all its aspects can thrive best. Nurture it, respect it, work hard to make it good and into something precious, into the best part of your lives. Rising above judgement of your partner's imperfections will make your bond stronger and your life even more fulfilled. In the end it is the give-and-take of a moral life that enables us to have the loving relationships we want and deserve.

References

Dr. Meg Jay, Univ. of Virginia: "On the Pros and Cons of Cohabitation", 2011

Sarah Wheeler: "The Magnetic North", 2009

Jay Buckley, Prof.of History, Brigham Young Univ.: "William Clark, Indian Diplomat", 2008

Dr. Christopher Ryan, Research Psychologist and Dr. Calcida Jetha, Practicing Psychiatrist: "Sex at Dawn", 2011

Dr. Margaret Farley: "Just Love - a Framework for Christian Sexual Ethics", 2006

Prof. Robert P. George, "The Conscience and its Enemies", Princeton, 2013

Dr. Dagmar Herzog, Prof. of Psychology, New York Univ.: "Sex in Crisis", 2009

Dr. Alex Comfort: "The Joy of Sex", 1972 and following editions

Dr. Amy Schalet, Prof. of Psychology, Univ. of Massachusetts: "Not under my Roof!", 2009

Dr. Barry Ginsberg, International Association of Marriage Counselors: "Improving Couples' Attachment Securities and Satisfaction", 2009

Vine Delorio: "Indians Of The Pacific Northwest", 2012

About The Author:

In his easy reading Essays on Morality, Dr. Wolfgang Mack takes a progressive and sometimes humorous look at today's Morality in our personal human behavior as well as in our political world. Starting with a survey of the historic developments of moral concepts the author takes us on a journey to show how our present-day Morality is constantly being shaped by the continual and rapid changes in our life circumstances and how the prevailing political environment has reacted. Dr. Mack shows us how life expectancy, technology, medicine, sociology and even theology have changed dramatically from the times of our ancestors, and how they caused new rules of moral behavior. But he also shows that some of the very fundamental issues of Morality that govern the ability for people living together in orderly communities will never change.

Born and raised in wartime Germany and trained in science and economics the author has managed industrial enterprises in several countries. In his work he guided the careers of many professionals from different parts of our world. Representing several industry associations in the halls of politicians and lawmakers he also gained insight into the often controversial Morality of interest groups attempting to influence our public policy making. He has lectured on a number of these subjects and served on many business and non-profit boards.

He lives in Seattle, Washington, married to his wife Francesca for over fifty years, enjoying their four sons and their families, and above all their eleven grandchildren who give special meaning to their lives.